I Go To Nursery School

Fiona Pragoff

METHUEN CHILDREN'S BOOKS

My name is Stacey.
I go to nursery school.
I like my nursery school.

I hang my coat on my peg.

It has my name on it and a picture of an elephant so that I know it's mine.

There are lots of things
to do at my nursery school.

You can
build a car.

You can cut
out pictures.

You can blow
shiny bubbles.

You can do
a puzzle.

You can make
a puppet.

You can
ring up.

You can look
at a book.

You can do
cooking.

Or you can . . .

. . . splash with water.
SPLASH!

Now it's milktime.
It's my turn to pour the milk!

Then I
drink mine
all up.

After milktime we play in
the garden.

Here are some of my friends
swinging on the rope ladder.

And now we all play
'Here we go round
the mulberry bush'
with our teacher.

When it's lunchtime we go
indoors.
First we wash our hands.

Then we get the tables ready.

I help to
put out
the cups.

Today we are having stew.
What vegetables do you see?

I'm having peas and carrots,

and one great big potato!

After lunch we clear
away our plates,

and then we clean our teeth.
Here are our toothbrushes.
They're all different colours.

What colour is
my toothbrush?

Some children have a sleep
after lunch,

but I'm going to feed our guinea pig, Snowy.

Bright green cabbage leaves are his favourite food.

Now we do some painting.
Let's paint our faces first.

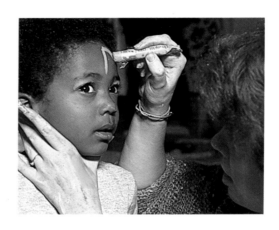

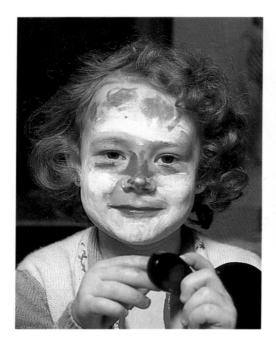

Then we paint a rainbow on the floor. Can you see the colours?

There's red and yellow,
blue and green!

Here are our paints and brushes.
One brush for each colour.

Sometimes we
paint with
our brushes
at an easel,

and sometimes we do handprints.

After we've
finished we
hang our
paintings
up to dry.

Now we play some music.

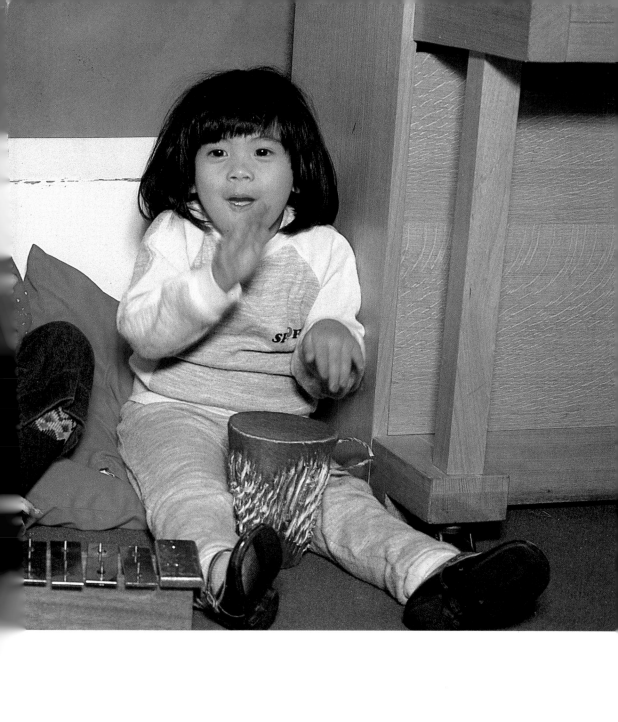

CRASH! My cymbals
make the loudest noise!

It's time to go home now.
I'm putting on my coat.

I've had a lovely day.
What will we do tomorrow,
I wonder?